Catalina Island

Gayle Baker, Ph.D.

Printed in Canada by Hignell Book Printing

Library of Congress Cataloging in Publication Data:

Baker, Gayle
  Catalina Island / Gayle Baker, Ph.D.
  1st ed. p. cm.
  Includes index.
  ISBN 0-9710984-0-9
  History of Santa Catalina Island, CA
  I. Title

PCN 2001090752

Cover by Larry Iwerks, renowned Santa Barbara water-colorist.

All historical photos are from the Catalina Island Museum

Table of Contents

Travel brochures from 1900, left, and 1930, right, above.

Luggage sticker from ferry.

What's So Special About Catalina Island?

Santa Catalina Island, the third largest of California's eight Channel Islands, is comprised of 47,844 acres and covers approximately 75 square miles. It is located 19.7 miles from the nearest mainland, Palos Verdes Peninsula. It is twenty-one miles long, with 54 miles of coastline. Approximately six miles from the westernmost end are two opposing coves that nearly cut Catalina in two. The thin neck of land remaining, called "Isthmus", is only ¼-mile wide. Early explorers believed they had discovered two islands when they saw Santa Catalina Island from sea.

Catalina Island is known for its marvelous climate and is often compared to the Mediterranean Riviera. In the summer, it is consistently ten degrees cooler than the mainland due to cool ocean breezes. During the winter, temperatures average ten degrees higher, as a result of the warm Japanese current that flows into the San Pedro Channel between Catalina and the mainland.

Catalina is a paradise for anglers, tourists, environmentalists, scuba divers, boaters, and beach-lovers alike, drawing over 1,000,000 visitors to its shores each summer. It is little wonder that some liken it to a modern-day Camelot.

In addition to its perfect climate and natural beauty, Catalina has a fascinating history. Alma Overholt, long-time Catalina resident, curator of The Catalina Island Museum, and author of a wonderful history of the Island, *The Catalina Story*, captured the magic of Catalina in a few words:

Perhaps no other similar area in the United States can equal its history of ancient cultures, high adventures of explorers, buccaneers and smugglers, mining and real estate booms, great game fishing, and down to the present day, a resort of world-renown.

Catalina is:

Home of the smartest, most trainable sealions. Most sealions performing throughout the world can trace their ancestry to Catalina Island.

Believed to be the first place in California that gold was discovered.

Location for the filming of many popular movies.

The birthplace of deep sea sport fishing and the world's first glass bottom boat.

Reputed home of a mysterious sea serpent much like the Loch Ness Monster.

A popular hideout for pirates of yesteryear and smugglers throughout the centuries.

Home to as many as four different tribal cultures.

The "Island of Love" romanticized in more than 30 songs and hundreds of poems.

And so much more. . . .

So turn the page, and begin your journey into Catalina's story with this unique *HarborTown History.*

Tribal Homeland

During the past two centuries, Catalina Island has been relatively unpopulated. This was not the case centuries ago when large numbers of Native Islanders called Catalina their home. Experts believe that as many as four different tribes have lived on Catalina during the past 30,000 years.

Although most of the information about Catalina's earliest tribes has been lost, archaeologists have discovered a great deal about the more recent tribes. Much of the evidence we have of them has been gathered from "middens"—ancient dumps where they tossed everything they no longer needed. These middens mark their settlements and have given archaeologists information about their diets and their habits. It has been estimated that there are more than 2000 middens on Catalina, only half of which have been discovered. One can still identify the locations of these ancient middens by finding soil that has been blackened by fish oil and littered with mounds of crumbling abalone shells. Even today, almost every time a foundation for a new building is dug on the Island, remains of her once-flourishing tribes can be found.

Evidence from these middens indicates that around 2000 B.C. as many as 2500 lived on Catalina Island at three major settlements, near today's Little Harbor, Avalon, and Two Harbors (Isthmus Cove and Cat Harbor). In addition to these major settlements, hundreds of other smaller sites have been located. Some or these smaller sites were permanent, while others served as temporary hunting and fishing bases.

There is much that is unknown about Catalina's Native Islanders. Our written knowledge of them did not begin until the Spanish arrived in 1542 and began chronicling their observations. Before their arrival, we have only theories based on the evidence that has been discovered from middens, burial grounds, and cave paintings. One of these theories is that Catalina was populated by a series of racially different groups.

Many believe that the first of these tribes were unusually tall. This is based on evidence gathered when burial grounds were excavated and looted in the 19th century. Many of the oldest and most deeply buried skeletons were over seven feet tall. By the time the Spanish arrived, there was no evidence of these extremely tall Islanders. There is evidence, though, that the people described by the Spanish were racially different from the tribes on the mainland. The Spanish described the people they found on Catalina as "fair and ruddy of complexion" and "white and blonde."

Experts question the origins of these different civilizations. Some believe that the Mongolians, who crossed the land bridge which connected Siberia and Alaska and settled much of the American continent, may have made Catalina their home. Some contend that Aztecs migrated north from South America to settle on the Island. Others maintain that Catalina tribes are the descendants of the Shoshonean tribes of the Great Basin. While it is possible that any or all of these groups settled on Catalina Island, none of these theories accounts for the evidence of the extraordinarily tall or of the fair, blonde Islanders. For now, these questions remain unanswered.

Life on Catalina

Experts agree that a pure form of the Stone Age existed on Catalina Island longer than anywhere else on the North American continent, with the possible exception of Canada. This is probably because soapstone, an easy-to-carve stone, was available in large quantities on the Island. This soapstone (also called steatite) was used to make bowls, mortars, pestles, and a variety of other implements for use and for barter with other tribes. In 1878, an archaeologist reported that he had located more than 300 soapstone quarries in a two-square-mile area in the middle of the Island.

An article in the **Los Angeles Times** in 1906 poetically described one of these soapstone quarries:

> *The largest workshop of the Indians lies far in the heart of Catalina and had never been disturbed. Here goats roam over trails which their little feet have worn smooth as satin, and kick out of their way many a precious thing the Indians chiseled.*
>
> *It is very strange, this magic. . . . There are tiny pots small enough to have been used as a child's bowl and others too heavy for a white man to lift! . . . You come across them in all stages, from the largest one not yet loosened from its base and still standing firmly two feet high, to the chiseled ones rounded and modeled so that a mere touch of hand or foot will set them rolling. . . .*

Catalina Native Islanders used lava to make weapons, and bones to make musical instruments. Shells were used to make fishhooks and hair ornaments and to decorate their bone flutes and pipes. They did not make pottery. They wove reeds and lined them with melted asphaltum to make watertight jugs and bowls. Most of the items that the Catalina tribes produced were for their own needs. They were, however, successful traders of jewelry and stone carvings. There is evidence that they traded these items with tribes as far away as Nevada and New Mexico.

Some Islanders lived in large circular huts that were sixty feet in diameter and covered with closely-woven mats. Each of these huts accommodated fifty people. Other groups lived in caves. Pictographs drawn in red ocher can still be found in some of these caves.

They ate fish, abalone, acorns, cactus, and a sweet potato-like root that they took to the mainland to barter. Acorns and cactus seeds were ground into meal and baked into a flat bread. During feasts, large fish would be cooked in a hole in the ground.

They crafted fine canoes made of pine planks lashed together with cordage made from red milkweed. These canoes were as long as twenty-five feet by four feet wide and carried from eight to ten people. According to the log of Viscaino, an early Spanish explorer:

> They have well-made canoes made of pine planks fastened together with thongs of sealskin. They have poops and bows like barks. Some of them are so large that 20 men can man them. They have double, sharp bladed paddles which they ply in unison on one side and the other. They go flying like the wind.

Records indicate that the Catalina tribes were regarded as fierce, sinister, and evil wizards by the mainland tribes. It is likely that their isolation, the threatening oceans they braved, and their dominance in the region's most important religious ceremonies gave them this air of power, prestige, and mystery.

The First Recorded Observations

When the Spanish arrived, their observations of the tribes living on Catalina were faithfully recorded. It is from their journals that we have our first written historical records of Catalina's Native Islanders.

In 1542, only fifty years after Columbus had first discovered America, General Rodriguez Cabrillo briefly anchored his ship in White's Landing, near Long Point, and recorded the following in his log:

> . . . when the boat came near, a great number of Indians emerged from the bushes and grass, shouting and dancing, and making signs that they should not be afraid. Immediately they were assured, they laid their bows and arrows on the ground and launched in the water a good canoe which held eight to ten Indians, and came to the ships. The Spaniards gave them beads and other articles

with which they were pleased. Afterwards the Spaniards went ashore and they and the Indian women and all, felt very secure. Here an old Indian made signs to them that men like the Spaniards, clothed and bearded, went about the mainland.

In addition to this rich description of the people of Catalina, this journal entry introduces a mystery that has never been solved: Who were these "men like the Spaniards, clothed and bearded?"

Sixty years after Cabrillo's brief visit, Catalina had a second visitor. On November 24, 1603, General Sebastian Viscaino arrived. He named the island Santa Catalina, after Saint Caterina, on whose day he had arrived. According to Viscaino's log:

The Indians are robust and well-made. The men are all naked. Their women are well shaped, have fine eyes and beautiful features. They are modest and wear clothing of sealskin from their breasts down. The boys and girls are white and blonde. All are affable and smiling.

The Islanders guided his ship into a safe anchorage and prepared a feast for the entire crew. Almost immediately, the Spanish began their attempts to convert them to Christianity. The day after their arrival, Viscaino and his crew built an altar on shore and a Mass was conducted at which "more than one hundred men and women were present. . . .They marveled not a little at seeing the altar and the image of our Lord Jesus crucified, and listened attentively to the saying of the Mass, asking by signs what it was about. They were told it was about heaven."

Religious Beliefs

In return for the invitation to the Spaniards' Mass, they honored Viscaino and his crew by allowing them to attend a ceremony in their awesome temple. The oldest, wisest, and most powerful leaders of tribes from the entire region came to this temple once a year to worship. According to an 1877 United States Geological Survey map, this temple was located on the flat meadow between Isthmus Cove and Cat Harbor. Here, ceremonies celebrating the important life events, including birth, puberty, marriage, and death, were performed. The eagle, raven, and rattlesnake were worshiped as reincarnated ancestors who had returned to earth to guard the living.

When Viscaino's soldiers attended the ceremony, one took a far more active role than anticipated. According to Viscaino's log:

> There was a great circle all surrounded with feathers which must have come from birds which had been sacrificed. Inside the circle there was an idol that resembled a demon painted in various colors. It had no head, but two horns and a dog at its feet. The sun and moon were painted in its sides. Eagle feathers were stuck to it, and on stakes around it, with asphaltum.
>
> The General told the Indians that the idol was evil, and placed the sign of the cross on it. When the soldiers arrived there were two huge crows inside the circle, larger than ordinary crows. One of the soldiers took aim with his harquebus and killed them both. At this time the Indians began to lament and show great emotion. In my opinion, the devil talked to them through these crows. I saw with my own eyes Indian women cleaning fish on the beach for food for their families. Some crows came up and with their bills took fish out of the hands with no protest from the Indian women.

Despite this killing of their sacred ravens, the Catalina tribes continued to welcome the explorers, hunters, and smugglers who frequented Catalina Island during the 17th and 18th centuries and the early years of the 19th century. Each brought changes and new diseases to their isolated culture.

In addition to the prestige the Catalina tribes received for building their great temple, they were also honored for initiating an important religious ceremony—the "Jimson Weed Cult." This ceremony initiated adolescent boys into manhood. The jimson weed is native to Catalina Island. It is an extremely potent narcotic that can make cattle seriously ill. Native Islanders dried the roots of this jimson weed and ground them into a powder. They brewed it with boiling water and gave it to young men who had fasted for three days. These adolescents danced until they passed out. Their dreams during this stupor were believed to be prophetic and to predict their future. Unfortunately, the jimson weed drink made many very ill and killed a number of these young men. As the source of this cult, the Catalina Native Islanders were viewed with awe and became the religious leaders of the region.

Death of a Civilization

In 1806, Captain Joseph O'Cain and his partner, Jonathan Winship, joined forces with the Russian-American Fur Company, based in Sitka, Alaska, to hunt otter. The luxurious furs of these gentle animals were used by Russian nobility for cloaks and were so prized that each skin brought $50 to $100. O'Cain and Winship planned to make a great deal of money very quickly by gathering as many skins as possible from the otter-rich waters of Catalina Island. The Russian-American Fur Company supplied O'Cain and Winship with one-hundred-and fifty Aleut hunters, bidarkas (canoes made of hides), and guns in exchange for a percentage of the profit. It is suspected that these Aleut hunters had been enslaved and forced to journey south for the otter kill. These Aleuts killed not only enormous numbers of otters, but also brutally looted, raped, and slaughtered the Catalina Native Islanders. Many who survived this brutal onslaught contracted a variety of diseases introduced by these Aleut hunters.

Catalina's Native Islanders never recovered. Between 1820 and 1832, hopeless and broken, those who still survived left the Island forever. They were relocated to the San Gabriel Mission. The result was the total demoralization of a once proud civilization. Those at the mission soon died of disease, poor diet, and, possibly, broken spirits. After thriving for centuries, a great civilization disappeared almost overnight. They left only an island rich with memories from a happier time.

Artifacts

During the last half of the 19th century, tourists entertained themselves by collecting relics as souvenirs, while archaeologists took these artifacts in the name of science. Much interest was focused on locating the great temple at Isthmus, for little remained to validate its existence. According to Paul Schumacher, in an **Overland Monthly** article published in 1875, the archaeologists were too late.

> *The archaeology of this island is said to have been ransacked by a scientific gentleman of merit, who lingered formerly around the picturesque isthmus. He told me himself, some time ago, that he had even spotted the. . . temple . . .To my deep regret, I found that there was but little left for our party to gather, and nothing new to science.*

No one knows who carried away all the relics of the great temple or why. Were the remains of this religious center taken as souvenirs or scientific discoveries? The result is the same: nothing remains of this great temple.

Today, some Catalina artifacts are on exhibit at the Heye Foundation Museum of the American Indians in New York. Others are in the Catalina Island Museum in the Casino at Avalon. Many more of the relics have been lost, destroyed, or forgotten. Little seems to remain of this once-thriving civilization.

Catalina Almost Became a Tribal Prison

During the Civil War, the Union army occupied Catalina Island. The captain in command, Captain West, believed Catalina would be an excellent reservation. When he shared this opinion with colleagues in Washington, Brigadier General Wright agreed and wrote the following to the Adjutant-General of the Army:

> *From a special report that I have just received from the officer commanding on the Island [West] I am well satisfied that it is better adapted for an Indian reservation than I at first supposed.*

Others agreed. James Curtis stated in his report of January 2, 1864: "No more fitting place could be found for a general hospital or depot for Indian prisoners." Orders were given to the Department of the Interior to begin the work needed to convert Catalina into a reservation.

Suddenly, Brigadier General Wright, who had initially supported this action, changed his recommendation. Action was put on hold, but, as late as 1886, Senator James Fair, the multi-millionaire owner of the Comstock Lode, wrote this letter to the Secretary of the Interior:

> *It (Catalina) is isolated and too far from shore for any ordinary boat to reach it. My idea is that if the Apaches were put on the island, they would require no guards, and all that would be required would be a small tender and crew to run between the island and Wilmington for the purpose of communication and supplies. This would, in my opinion, set the Apache question at rest forever, and would save the country many valuable lives, and the government millions in money.*

The **Los Angeles Herald** responded that Catalina was "too good for the proposed occupants" for, in the ensuing years, Catalina had soared in value. During the second half of the 19th century, Catalina had become the focus of many dreams as speculators and developers competed for ownership of the Island. A complex succession of entrepreneurs purchased Catalina Island—each willing to pay more. As prices rose and plans for commercializing Catalina grew, the ideas of turning the Island into a reservation or an Apache prison were forgotten.

Catalina had become a piece of valuable real estate and was never to be a tribal homeland again. Thankfully, it was never to become a prison or reservation, either.

Despite this total exodus of Catalina's Native Islanders, if one climbs high into the hills of Little Harbor and looks down, one can still envision the vanished civilization that lived, loved, worshiped, and died on this incredible island known to us as Santa Catalina Island.

Spanish Explorers, Trappers, and Smugglers Discover Catalina Island

The Arrival of the Spanish

Catalina Island was discovered many years before most of the rest of the country. Cabrillo described two islands and, for many years, historians believed that he had seen both Catalina and San Clemente Islands. There is now general agreement that he had been confused by the low land at Isthmus and believed that he was viewing two separate, adjacent islands. He anchored his ship in White's Landing near Long Point, gave the Native Islanders beads, claimed Catalina Island for Spain, and continued to explore California's coast.

Sixty years after Cabrillo's brief stay at Catalina, a second Spanish explorer, General Sebastian Viscaino, arrived. On November 24, 1602, he anchored near the Isthmus and named the Island for Saint Caterina.

Although both Cabrillo and Viscaino made only brief visits to Catalina, they provided the first written records of the Island and her people. They also led the parade of many who came to Catalina to use her resources and profit from her location. Trappers, smugglers, ranchers, miners, and entrepreneurs came to Catalina, seeking wealth from this natural paradise less than twenty miles across the San Pedro Channel from the mainland.

The Spanish claimed ownership of Catalina Island and tried to control it. They had, however, neither the personnel nor the resources to accomplish this. As trappers and smugglers discovered the value of Catalina, it became more and more difficult for the Spanish to exert any control over the activities on the Island. For centuries, trapping and illegal trading thrived there.

The Trappers

For awhile, trappers found instant wealth in Catalina's abundant and easy-to-trap otter. With the exception of the ruthless killing spree by the large group of Aleut hunters, most trappers arrived alone or in small groups. They traveled quickly, lightly, and quietly. The Spanish had a very difficult time finding and controlling them. Nevertheless, the Spanish authorities resented these trappers who were making such good profits from killing their otters.

They made it as difficult as they could for trappers to travel and trap in the area. When the well-known trapper, Jedediah S. Smith, arrived in San Diego, he was held prisoner for several months before well-respected citizens convinced the government that he was harmless and peaceful. When he was finally released he went to Catalina where he trapped otter for two days before moving on.

Although these solitary hunters did not loot or kill the Native Islanders, as had the Aleuts, they still left a bloody legacy: they brought disease to the tribes on the Island and exterminated the otter population.

The Smugglers

Soon, the trappers needed a new source of income. Almost simultaneously, the Spanish imposed extremely high duties on trading. In need of income, many trappers saw these duties as an opportunity to turn to smuggling for their income. Already familiar with her isolation, well-hidden coves, and safe anchorages, smugglers selected Catalina as their safe haven and the Island's chapter as a smugglers' paradise began.

For two centuries, innumerable treasures, from pirate's booty to bootlegger's alcohol, have been successfully hidden on Catalina Island.

By the early 1800s, smuggling was flourishing all along the coast.

The Spanish had clearly lost their battle to control California. Soon, smuggling was so common that even reputable ship captains and wealthy traders routinely smuggled goods up and down the California coast. According to Sir George Simpson, a respected trader:

> These probationary exactions (125% of the value of the merchandise) defeat their object, by the encouragement they afford to smuggling, three-fourths of the goods introduced into the country being run ashore, and the remaining one-fourth only passing through customs.

Richard Henry Dana observed and documented smuggling on Catalina in his famous, best-selling book, **Two Years Before the Mast**. He told the world how most of the vessels arriving in California hid their cargo on Catalina Island. A very small portion of this cargo was taken to Monterey to be declared and taxed. When the taxed portion had been sold, the ship was restocked in Catalina with the untaxed cargo. Ships continued trading up and down the coast and restocking at Catalina Island until all of the illegal cargo had been sold.

One of Catalina's most famous smugglers was the dashing, twenty-three year old co-owner of the **Lela Byrd**, Captain William Shaler. In 1803, he reached San Diego in need of wood and water. His ship was full of illegal otter skins. Spanish authorities suspected he was smuggling, and a skirmish began. Shaler escaped. No one was hurt, but his ship was damaged. He took his smuggled otter skins to China, where they brought excellent prices.

By the following year, the **Lela Byrd** was leaking badly, but Shaler wanted more profit before taking the time to repair his ship. According to Shaler:

> The 14th of March, I paid a visit to the island of Santa Catalina . . . and I determined that, after collecting all the skins on the coast, I would return to it and careen the ship [rest it on its side on the sand], which she was by this time greatly in want of. After completing our business on the coast, we returned to Santa Catalina, and anchored in the harbor on the first of May.

The Catalina Native Islanders enthusiastically welcomed Shaler and helped with the repairs. Six weeks later, the *Lela Byrd* was freshly caulked with lime and pitch and ready to cross the Pacific again. En route to Canton, Shaler came across a deal he could not refuse. Despite the exorbitant profits awaiting him in China, he sold his ship and all his otter skins to the king of the Sandwich Islands. Shaler never sailed again. Instead, he accepted a post as Consul for Havana, Cuba and remained there until his death from cholera in 1833 at the age of fifty-five.

When the Mexican government took over California, the high duties were not lowered. Instead, in addition to these high taxes, a law was passed that required that all coastal trading be done in Mexican vessels. If anything, this increased smuggling activities rather than stopping them. Two incidents involving Captains Cunningham and Bradshaw illustrate how ineffective the Mexican government was in its attempts to control smuggling:

1) In 1826, Cunningham and Bradshaw erected a hut on Catalina to protect their smuggled cargo. The Mexican government ordered them to tear it down. They replied promptly and reported that the hut had been destroyed. They were not telling the truth. This same hut, known later as Bradshaw's Hut, was still standing as late as 1886.

2) Two years later, the Governor of Mexico accused Bradshaw of a variety of illegal acts, including smuggling on Catalina Island. He was ordered to unload his cargo so that it could be examined. Instead, Bradshaw cut the cable that secured his ship and sailed safely out of port under a barrage of Mexican gunfire.

Smuggling changed, but did not end, when the United States gained control of California in 1848. High taxes were repealed, and it was no longer profitable to hide cargoes in the Island's coves. However, laws were soon passed that made it very profitable to smuggle people.

In 1882, the United States passed the China Exclusion Act that was designed to prohibit Chinese from entering the United States and to deport any Chinese who were already here. Ship captains were paid well to transport Chinese back to China.

Chinese workers were needed for the hard labor of building of railroads and railroad owners were unwilling to lose these hard workers. They were determined to keep their Chinese workers and looked to the same ship captains for help. The plan: Chinese workers were deported, as the law required. They were only taken as far as Catalina Island before they were smuggled into America again. Ship captains hid their human cargo on the Island in camps that sprang up all over the Island. (China Point was named for one of these camps.) At night, they smuggled these Chinese workers back into America through one of the three unguarded California ports: San Diego, San Pedro, or Monterey.

Ship captains had found an unending source of income—while they were being paid by the government to take deported Chinese back to China, they were also being paid handsomely by the railroads to smuggle the same people back into California. As this cycle continued, captains got richer and richer.

When Prohibition became a law in 1919, Catalina again became a smuggler's hideaway. Catalina's caves hid tons of bootlegged whiskey. Most of the bootleggers were not apprehended, for Catalina provided a perfect spot for bootlegging activities. Bootleggers with powerful lights hid on Catalina's hilltops and, when the coast was clear, signaled to the powerboats in the Island's coves which were loaded with illegal whiskey. These high-speed boats darted across the Channel to unload their alcohol on one of many deserted beaches on the mainland.

In 1923, one thousand cases of illegal whiskey were discovered near Eagle Rock. Pleasure boaters were warned to stay far from Eagle Rock until the bootleggers had been found.

For centuries, Catalina Island has provided a smugglers' haven for cargoes, people, and whiskey. No one knows how many rich caches of drugs have also been safely hidden in Catalina's coves. Some suspect there have been many. In 1966, a group of Explorer Scouts camping on the beach discovered a half-buried chest containing opium wrapped in gold leaf. How many other illegal secrets are still hidden in Catalina's coves—remnants of her rich history as a smugglers' paradise?

Hopes for Gold

During the 18th and 19th centuries, a parade of trappers and smugglers had profited from Catalina's resources. By the second half of the 19th century, it appeared that Catalina could offer an entirely new source of wealth – gold. Tales of rich veins of gold encouraged a new group of adventurers to journey to Catalina with hopes of mining her riches.

Stories of the search for gold on Catalina often star three men: George Yount, Samuel Prentiss, and Stephen Bouchette. Yount, Prentiss, and Louis Bouchette, Stephen's father, had hunted otter in Catalina's waters together for years. Yount and Prentiss had a secret that they shared with no one, not even each other.

The stories of these three men and their visions of gold have been told and retold for generations. With each retelling, these tales have become more interesting until fiction has become so interwoven with fact that no one is quite sure what really happened. The stories of these three men comprise an important Catalina legend. Much of it is even true.

George Yount arrived in California in 1830. During the next few decades, he made many trips to Catalina with Prentiss and Louis Bouchette in pursuit of otter. On one of his first trips, he picked up some quartz that appeared to contain gold deposits. He slipped it into his pocket and promptly forgot it. When enormous quantities of gold were found in Sutter's Creek, igniting the California Gold Rush of 1849, George began to wonder whether the sample he had found eighteen years earlier on Catalina Island had been gold. He made a number of trips to the Island, trying to locate another promising sample. He was unsuccessful each time. He made his last trip in 1854.

Discouraged after his last unsuccessful trip, he told some miners about the promising sample he had found years before. His timing was perfect. By this time, gold was beginning to become scarce in the Sutter's Creek region. Experienced prospectors were looking for new, rich fields. They listened to Yount's story and dreams of a rich gold vein on the Island began.

Samuel Prentiss, Yount's partner, spent a good bit of his life pursuing a different form of gold on Catalina—an unbelievably rich buried treasure. He and his other partner, Louis Bouchette, had the dubious distinction of being survivors of the first known shipwreck in San Pedro's history. After the wreck, they walked to the San Gabriel Mission for shelter. While living at the mission, Prentiss befriended Turai, who had been a chief of one of the powerful tribes on Catalina Island. Just before Turai died, he told Prentiss about a treasure buried on the Island and gave him a rough map of its location.

Prentiss returned to San Pedro. Using salvage from the wrecked ship, he built himself a small boat and headed for Catalina. Winds were strong. Most of his supplies were washed overboard, and he feared for his life. He reached Catalina, but the treasure map was gone. He had not memorized the map and had no idea where to search. He only remembered that the treasure was buried under a tree. Legend has it that Prentiss spent thirty years searching for this treasure by chopping down tree after tree and digging underneath each one. He built himself a cabin at Emerald Bay and survived by fishing, hunting otter, and selling firewood from the trees he was continually chopping down.

Prentiss died in 1854 without ever having found his treasure. He was the first non-Native Islander to live permanently on Catalina and to be buried there. Indications are that he was buried near Howland's Landing. In 1864, a wanderer exploring the hills of Catalina had this to say about what is believed to be Prentiss's final resting-place:

> *The only grave I saw on the Island was at this place. Opposite his [Howland's] residence, scarcely a furlong*

distant, on a pleasant slope near the seashore, is a solitary grave, surrounded by pickets painted dark brown. The lonely occupant of that small enclosure doubtless sleeps well. I looked upon it, and sighed, wondering if his days had been spent toiling—mining—or busy trade; envied the lot of the sleeper, and passed on to the shore, to hold communion with the deep, dark, rolling, restless sea.

A tablet, erected many years later by Judge Banning, still marks the site of Prentiss' Emerald Bay cabin with this inscription:

> *In memory of Samuel Prentiss*
> *A native of Massachusetts*
> *Came to California in 1824*
> *Died on Catalina 1854—Age 72*

Just before Prentiss died in 1854, he told **Stephen Bouchette**, son of his partner, Louis, about the treasure. Bouchette began the search for the treasure immediately. His timing was excellent. He began his search for gold the same year (1854) that Yount had told the experienced prospectors about his belief that Catalina had rich gold resources. As soon as the prospectors from the goldfields to the north began to arrive, Bouchette staked a claim and announced that he had found a rich vein of gold in the hills of Catalina.

Before long, he got financial backing, opened the Mineral Hills Mines Company, and was soon successfully mining silver, lead, and gold. More than $10,000 was spent for extensive tunnels that stretched over 800 feet. (These tunnels have caved in and are now filled with water.) Bouchette mined for many years and was even mentioned in a 1926 edition of *Scientific American* for his innovative tunnels, rails, and dump carts.

Despite his successful mining operation, Bouchette's passion was still with Turai's lost treasure. During the years that the Mineral Hills Mines Company operated, he borrowed money from the mine so that he could continue digging under trees for the treasure Prentiss had never found. Some believe his mines never had rich gold veins and that he had claimed rich mineral discoveries only to get investors to unknowingly finance his treasure hunt. To this day, no one knows whether the Mineral Hills Mines Company was a rich stake or a hoax.

On one trip to the mainland, Bouchette married a French girl from a dance hall. In an attempt to keep her happy on the isolated Island, he built her an elegant mansion near Emerald Bay. He furnished it with English mahogany furniture and French plate glass mirrors. One day in 1878, he and his wife loaded silver ore and provisions onto a sailboat and were never seen again. Did his wife insist on returning to the mainland? After twenty-four years, was he simply tired of searching for treasure? Or, had they found the buried treasure at long last?

Catalina Island's Gold Rush

Although a few had been quietly searching the hills of Catalina for gold for many years, it was not until 1863 that a stampede of gold seekers flooded Catalina to stake their claim and find their fortune. The first mines were located at Fourth of July Cove, Cherry Cove, and Mineral Hill. All of these claims were within five miles of the Isthmus. According to one miner:

> The claims laid out are almost innumerable. Scarcely any regard has been paid to the original locators. Litigation will be abundant, provided the mines prove rich, to settle conflicting interests. Many tunnels have been run from twenty-five to fifty feet and abandoned.

To avoid the impending chaos, the miners established the San Pedro Mining District, a large area that spanned all of the Channel Islands. By April 1863, they had developed the "Mining Laws of San Pedro Mining District." These "laws" were actually a set of agreements concerning claims. These codes limited the size of a claim to 600 linear feet and the duration of claim to six months. The only way to continue a claim was to work the claim for six days each month after the first six months.

Founders of the San Pedro Mining District also began planning a city at Emerald Bay to be named Queen City. Lots were staked out and maps were drawn, but nothing was actually built at Catalina's Queen City. Instead, settlements at Fourth of July and Cherry Cove sprang up quickly. The town at Fourth of July Cove, named Glen Haven:

> *contains eight dwelling houses, two tents, two workshops, and several out-door forges for sharpening picks. Its inhabitants number three ladies, thirty miners, no children. There is neither horse, cart, cow, nor grog shop in Glen Haven, but its mineral wealth can scarcely be estimated. On each side of the Fourth of July Valley . . . are to be seen holes and tunnels without number.*

> *Cherry Cove, half a mile westerly from Glen Haven, is larger and pleasanter, and rivals it in mineral wealth. It numbers about forty men, without a woman or a child among them. It, however, boasts one store, kept by Mr. Fried, lately of San Francisco, and one grog shop, where thirsty souls may drink and yet be ever dry.*

In less than a year, almost 100,000 feet of claims were registered, and approximately 70 miners were actively mining these claims. Galena was discovered in addition to gold, silver, and copper. Activity was intense as miners worked their claims. All of this work was done manually, for these miners had no machinery to lighten their load. According to a California mineralogist's report, "no systematic development has ever been undertaken."

Prospectors focused on their vision of gold. They endured dangers and were content to live without conveniences until they had made their fortunes.

Despite the hardships during those mining days on Catalina Island, the prospectors enjoyed one convenience: Homing pigeons delivered their messages to the mainland in 45 minutes. When compared to the ten days it took in 1864 for a message to be delivered by mail from Isthmus to Wilmington, the significance of this convenience is clear. Even today, the Avalon Post Office does not match the air mail service enjoyed by the miners. Records indicate that pigeons were used to deliver messages for Catalina residents as late as 1899.

Miners Evicted

Catalina's gold boom was over almost before it began.

The United States was being torn apart by its bloody Civil War. Union leaders counted on shipments of gold from the mines in the Sutter's Creek area to finance their army. Some believed this gold was as essential to victory as were successful outcomes on the battlefields. It was rumored that Confederate leaders held the same opinion and were making plans to hijack the gold while it was en route from San Francisco to Washington, D.C.

Catalina, known as a smugglers' paradise, was identified as the perfect location for Confederates to hide out while waiting to hijack a rich gold shipment. When miners engulfed Catalina, Union leaders believed that many of them were only masquerading as miners – they were really waiting to hijack Union gold.

Based upon these rumors, but without evidence, the Union Army took possession of Catalina Island. Late in 1863, only six months after the first wave of prospectors had arrived and staked their claims, the Union Army built a garrison at Isthmus. Under the command of Captain West, the Army acted quickly to clear the Island of all civilians. West ordered all except the few ranchers who were raising stock on the Island to leave immediately. The miners were outraged and refused to leave their promising claims. They were convinced that the government was evicting them so that they could start mining their claims. On February 5, 1864, Captain West issued a second order to vacate the Island. This time, armed Union troops delivered the order.

Miners Capitulate and Leave Catalina.

As soon as the miners had left, the Union Army settled into its new location at Isthmus. They built a well, a windmill, and a barracks, all

28

of which still remain. (The barracks is currently occupied by the Isthmus Yacht Club.) Miners' shanties were destroyed, and Isthmus was renamed Union Bay. Of the miners, only Stephen Bouchette was allowed to stay because he could prove that he had legally purchased his property. According to a June 1864 article by the editor of San Francisco's **Daily Alta California**:

> *The Isthmus is almost entirely occupied by the military now stationed there. Captain West, the officer in command of the island, is a quiet, estimable gentleman, and a genial companion. His mild but firm discipline has endeared him to his men. Barracks are in the process of erection, and it would be wisdom in the Government to be liberal in its apportionment for military improvements on the island of Santa Catalina.*

The Union Army occupied Catalina for only a brief period. By September 20, 1864, less than a year after their arrival, they had left. In less than a century, the Native Islanders had left; traders and trappers were gone; smuggling was in a lull; miners had been evicted; and the Union soldiers had packed up and gone home. Catalina Island was empty and ready for the first group in the parade of entrepreneurs seeking her wealth.

Is There Gold on Catalina Island?

Hopes for rich gold deposits lived long after the banishment of the miners. Possibly, if the miners had been allowed to stay, it soon would have become clear that there was little gold on the Island. As it was, visions of this gold persisted for decades and fueled many lucrative Catalina real estate deals.

As soon as the Civil War was over, developers and investors began competing for ownership of Catalina. Using the promise of a gold-rich bonanza, speculators invested and the value of Catalina real estate rose rapidly. In 1873, Max Stroble almost sold Catalina Island to a group of gold-seeking English investors for the enormous price of a million dollars, but he died before the deal was completed.

Several years later another English syndicate with visions of a gold-rich Pacific island paradise paid George Shatto $400,000 for the right to begin mining.

Even during the 20th century, hopes for Catalina's mineral wealth flourished. William Wrigley, Jr., the chewing gum magnate and Catalina's most famous owner, began mining on Catalina in 1923. He was curious about all of the tales of great wealth in Catalina's hills. He was also seeking employment opportunities for Catalina's residents. He began a mining operation on Black Jack Mountain where lead and zinc had already been discovered.

Silver, lead, and zinc were found with assays as high as $347 per ton. Silver, up to 200 ounces per ton, was also found. With these promising assay results, a second mine was developed just above Pebbly Beach. An additional floating mill was built at White's Landing. A road was constructed from Mt. Black Jack to the mill, and a pier was built. Ore was shipped to San Francisco and Belgium. In 1924, more than $100,000 worth of lead, zinc, and silver was mined.

Wrigley's Catalina mining operations were just swinging into high gear when the price of metals dropped so dramatically that it was no longer profitable to mine Catalina's hills. By 1927, the mines had been abandoned, and the floating mill dismantled. Mining has not been attempted again on Catalina Island, but, as Philip K. Wrigley said,"When the time comes that we need them [Catalina's minerals], we know where they are."

Catalina's Owners and Their Dreams

Following her years as the homeland of many Native Islanders, Catalina was claimed by a long succession of owners. Each had a markedly different vision for her. Catalina's first owners were nations. The Spanish claimed the Island in 1542. For almost three centuries, Spain tried to control the activities on Catalina Island and failed. During the 19th century, the ownership of Catalina passed from Spain to Mexico (in 1821) and then to the United States (in 1848). Each brought a different set of laws, expectations, and dreams for the Island.

Once the United States gained ownership, a parade of individuals purchased Catalina. These owners changed even more frequently than the countries that had claimed her. **Thomas Robbins** was the first in a succession of citizens who tried to own Catalina. Of these owners of Catalina Island, Robbins was the only one who did not offer to buy her. He found another way to acquire Catalina Island.

Robbins, an American from Massachusetts, was the owner of a general store in Santa Barbara and the captain of a schooner operated by the Mexican government. During his many visits to Catalina, he began to dream of owning the Island and ranching there. In 1839, he petitioned the Mexican governor of California, asking for Catalina. His petition was denied.

His luck began to change when he became the friend of Pio Pico, the last Mexican governor of California before it became an American territory. Robbins and Pio Pico shared a love for Catalina, for Pio Pico had enjoyed many hunting and pleasure excursions to the Island. When Robbins asked Pio Pico for Catalina, his timing was perfect: Mexico and the United States were at war, and it was obvious that Mexico would soon lose all of California. Robbins asked for Catalina as Pio Pico was fleeing California and staying at Robbins' home. Pio Pico gave Robbins Catalina on July 4, 1846. According to legend, he wrote the grant on a crumbled piece of butcher paper in exchange for a fresh horse and silver saddle. It was his last official act as the Mexican governor of California. Three days later, on July 7, 1846, Mexican rule ceased.

The United States formally gained ownership of Catalina in 1848 in the Treaty of Guadaloupe-Hidalgo that ended the war between Mexico and the United States. Robbins was convinced that he held a legal claim to Catalina Island and built a home on the Island. By 1847, he had begun cultivating land, had built a corral, and had acquired some cattle.

His dream did not last for long. By 1850, Robbins had sold Catalina to a friend, **Don Jose Covarrubias**, for $10,000. By 1853, Covarrubias had lost interest in Catalina and sold it to **Albert Packard**. Records show that Albert purchased Catalina for the unbelievable price of $1,000. Although there are no records confirming it, many believe Covarrubias received unrecorded goods or services in addition to the money from Packard.

An interesting footnote to Robbins' rather short-lived ownership of Catalina: years later the United States District Court declared that Robbins had never owned Catalina. According to a report sent to the Attorney General of the United States on February 17, 1857:

> It is . . . with extreme reluctance I recommend its dismissal. The whole evidence in its entirety and parts I take to be meager and incomplete to say nothing concerning the question of fraud arising out of the documents and Testimony in the case.

By the time this ruling was handed down, Catalina had been sold by Robbins, sold by Don Jose Covarrubias, and was currently held by Albert Packard. All of these sales and purchases were based upon the false assumption that Robbins had legally owned Catalina.

Despite the ruling invalidating Packard's legal ownership of

Catalina, he sold the Island in 1864 to **James Ray** for $12,500. Ray kept one-quarter and split up the rest of the Island into parcels and offered to sell them. A mere nine days after Ray had bought Catalina, he sold one-half of the Island to **James Lick** for $4150.

Lick's Ownership of Catalina

Lick was one of Catalina's most interesting owners. He was very different from many of the flamboyant entrepreneurs of his time. He had arrived in San Francisco in 1847 with $40,000. While the miners searched for gold, he bought land in the thriving city. In 1861, he built a magnificent mansion, the Lick House. He immediately rented it, and lodged in one of its cheapest rooms. Even after he became wealthy and had an annual income over $200,000, he continued to travel in a decrepit buggy pulled by his old, tired horse. While people made fun of him, he got richer and richer. In Los Angeles, he purchased prime real estate, the Los Feliz Rancho. This ranch is now Griffith Park.

Although he spent nothing on himself, he gave a good bit of his money away. He supported a library association, an old ladies' home, an orphans' shelter, free public baths, and a society for the prevention of cruelty to animals. His most famous legacy is the Lick Observatory, a powerful telescope on Mt. Hamilton near San Jose, operated by the University of California, Santa Cruz. When he died in 1876, he was buried beneath the dome of his powerful telescope.

The one-half of the Island Lick had obtained was just a start. He wanted to own all of Catalina. He immediately began negotiations to gain control of the rest of the Island. Before long, he was successful in purchasing an additional one-quarter of the Island but Lick still needed to obtain the final one-quarter owned by James Ray. James Ray got involved in a legal battle concerning the ownership of his portion. Lick waited and watched. In November 1866, Ray's portion went to **James Hawxhurst**. Lick saw his chance, and, by December of that year, Lick had obtained Hawxhurst's portion for $4140. After spending $27,150 and waiting three years, Lick owned all of Catalina.

As soon as Lick owned Catalina, he began marketing it to foreign investors as California's next rich gold field. Had he been more successful in selling Catalina to mining speculators, Catalina would not be the island paradise it is today.

In 1872, three investors, Major Max Stroble, John Downey, and John Forster, offered Lick $125,000 for Catalina. These investors planned to resell Catalina to Europeans and net a healthy profit. For a time, it looked as if they would accomplish just that. Major Stroble, a German winemaker, real estate promoter, and journalist went to London in 1873 to collect money from investors. He had formed a syndicate of English investors ready to invest heavily in the promise of the rich minerals buried in Catalina's hills. According to Harris Newmark:

> *The last grand effort of his adventurous spirit was the attempt to sell Santa Catalina Island. . . .Liberally supplied with rich mineral specimens, he negotiated the sale to a syndicate of London capitalists for one million dollars. . . .On the morning that the papers were to be signed and the money [$200,000] exchanged to close the deal, no Stroble kept the tryst to carry out his part in the transaction. Only the evening before, alone and unattended, the old man died in his room at the very moment when Fortune, for the first time, was to smile upon him!*

Avalon, the Birth of a Resort Town

Lick died soon after this deal fell through, and in 1887 his trustees sold Catalina to **George R. Shatto** and his agent, **C. A. Sumner**, for $200,000: $70,000 down and a mortgage of $130,000. Shatto and Sumner did not want to mine Catalina. They had dreams of transforming the Island into a world-class resort. They began by developing Catalina's first town. Its name, Avalon, was selected from Tennyson's ***Idylls of the King***. According to the Arthurian legend, when King Arthur was dying, he said that he was going to a paradise:

". . . to the island-valley of Avalon:
Where falls not hail, or rain, or any snow,
Nor ever wind blows loudly; but it lies
Deep-meadow'd, happy, fair with orchard lawnd
And bowery hollows crowned with summer sea,
Where I will heal me of my grievous wound."

Shatto and Sumner platted the streets of Avalon and began to sell lots. Prices for these lots ranged from $500 to $2000 each. Few of these lots were sold. Nevertheless, many came to Avalon for their holidays. They were able to pay $25 a year to rent a twenty-foot lot. They pitched tents or built flimsy cottages and came each year to Avalon to play. A small wharf was built and a steamer, owned and operated by the Bannings, came to Catalina twice a week to bring the ever-growing number of tourists.

Tent city in Avalon

Holly Hill House

Avalon's oldest remaining structure, the Holly Hill House, the home with the dome-shaped roof overlooking Avalon Bay, was built on a lot purchased for $500 from Shatto and Sumner. In 1888, **Peter Gano**, the engineer who built Catalina's first freshwater system, purchased this choice parcel of land and began building his home. He built the entire home by himself with help from Mercury, an old circus horse. He brought all of his building materials from the mainland on his boat, the *Osprey,* and designed a cable-car system to carry his equipment and supplies up the hill. On command, Mercury walked down the hill, drawing the loaded car uphill by ropes running through pulleys.

Holly Hill House with Sugar Loaf Rocks in background

Gano was a gifted craftsman who used only the finest materials. He was also a creative engineer who designed a system so that both groundwater and rainwater were used for daily water needs.

According to legend, he built this home for the woman he loved. In 1889 when it was complete, he asked her to come to him. She refused. She would not live on an island. Gano had to leave his home or lose his love. With hopes that she would relent, Gano remained in his home on Catalina. He named his home Lookout Cottage and waited. She eventually married someone else, and he lived in his wonderful home alone. It is said that, in his later years, he had signs posted around the property stating "No Women Allowed."

It is now called the Holly Hill House because of the holly growing on its hill. In 1971, a land company bought it with plans to build condominiums on the hill below. When excavation began, the foundation of the house became unstable. Work on the condominiums stopped immediately, and much money and energy were expended to make the foundation stable once again. The same year, Holly Hill House was sold to a couple with dreams of restoring it to its original beauty and making it their home. After extensive renovations, it is much like it was when Gano had so lovingly built it.

Avalon's First Hotels

To be a world-class resort, Avalon needed more than tourist tents and a few summer cottages. Thus, the Hotel Metropole, Catalina's first hotel, was built. Workmen were brought from the mainland to construct the hotel. According to Sumner, they were not particularly happy working on the Island: "Carpenters kicked because they could not get beef every day; plumbers objected to fresh fish and eggs; . . .and the roustabouts swore all the mutton was goat."

The Hotel Metropole was built on a flat lot overlooking Avalon Bay. This site had been a tribal settlement. As the foundation was being built, hundreds of artifacts were discovered. According to Sumner, "everyone that happened by took what he wanted." This hotel soon became a favorite place for the rich and famous. It looked as if Shatto and Sumner's dreams of turning Catalina into a world-renowned resort were about to become a reality.

But costs to develop Avalon were high, and Sumner still owed the Lick estate $130,000. Investors were solicited. Conservative English investors paid $100,000 toward the purchase price of $400,000 to mine Catalina's hills. Additional investors were sought to help pay the remaining $300,000. With this investment income, Shatto and

Hotel Metropole

Sumner felt that prosperity was just around the corner. Flushed with his dreams of wealth, Shatto spent $40,000 received from the English investors on a showy Los Angeles residence. He counted on future installments to meet his debt of $130,000 to the Lick estate and for the debts incurred for the development at Avalon. An English promoter, Smith, spent the remaining $60,000 on elaborate maps, surveys, a chartered boat to bring investors to Catalina, and plenty of champagne for these prospective investors.

This time, the public was simply not buying. Soon Shatto and Sumner were out of money and Smith was heading home to England, broke.

Captain William Banning, who had been operating the boats that had been bringing visitors to Catalina twice a week for years, watched as Shatto and Sumner headed for bankruptcy. His investment was threatened. Also, he had just realized that he wanted to be Catalina's next owner. When he decided he wanted Catalina, he wasted little time making it happen.

The Banning Years (1892-1919)

Captain William Banning wanted to obtain Catalina Island for a variety of reasons. First, he needed Catalina's rock to build a breakwater at Wilmington. Without this breakwater, he could not expand his shipping business. His family had made their fortune providing transportation. His father, General Phineas Banning, had become wealthy linking the cities of Southern California by stagecoach. William Banning and his brothers had made their fortune by establishing the Wilmington Transportation Company, Southern California's leading shipping company. They needed a breakwater at Wilmington to expand their business. The Bannings knew the seaside cliffs of Catalina Island would provide the best, cheapest source of rock for this breakwater.

The Bannings would also profit if Catalina became a world-class tourist resort. They owned the boats that brought tourists to the Island. As it appeared that Shatto and Sumner were going to be successful in transforming Avalon into a tourist haven, the Bannings had spent a great deal of their money building a luxurious new

SS Hermosa

yacht, the **Hermosa**, to bring even more visitors to the Island. If Catalina did not become a popular resort, the Bannings would lose money.

As he watched Shatto and Sumner struggle to hold on to Catalina, William Banning began to wonder why his profits should be limited to ferry fares. Why shouldn't the Bannings earn a double profit by owning the entire Island? Tourists would pay for the boat ride across the Channel. When they arrived, they would spend money on Banning-owned recreational activities.

The Bannings' need for a good source of rock, their financial commitment to Catalina's ferry service, and their financial savvy combined to make Catalina a very appealing business proposition for them. In addition to these solid financial reasons for obtaining the Island, Captain William Banning liked Catalina and wanted to have the opportunity to develop it into a recreational paradise. Once Banning decided he wanted to own Catalina Island, he did not want to wait for Shatto and Sumner to go bankrupt. He decided to see what could be done to force them out quickly.

> He whipped up his mule-team and drove splashing through the mud to his office at 222 West Second Street, Los Angeles. Here he gave quick orders to his secretary, Frank H. Lowe: "Draw a thousand dollars from the bank and catch the first boat out of New York. Get to London." Lowe was told to make his own decisions. If it appeared that Catalina was unavailable for purchase, Lowe was instructed to sell the steamer, **Hermosa**, before all development at Avalon ended. Lowe left in November of 1889. The day before Christmas that same year, Banning received a cable from him stating "The Island is yours."

Lowe devised a plan for obtaining Catalina. He sent each of the English investors who had promised to purchase Catalina's mineral rights from Shatto and Sumner an advertisement stating:

> "For sale: for $126,000, the Island of Santa Catalina, twenty-one miles off the coast of Southern California."

When they saw that they were paying far more for the mineral rights to Catalina than the entire Island was worth on the open market, they were, naturally, very upset. They met immediately. They saw no sense in continuing to pay for the mineral rights to an island that seemed to have so little value. They immediately dissolved their partnership and declared their agreement with Shatto and Sumner null and void. As soon as Lowe had sent his cable to Banning, he left England before anyone could ask him how he could advertise to sell an island he did not even own.

When the English investors forfeited their option to purchase Catalina's mineral rights, Shatto and Sumner were unable to meet their mortgage payments to the Lick estate. By 1892, Catalina had been sold to William Banning for $128,740. Before the deal was complete, Shatto was killed when his neck was broken in a train accident. Banning paid Shatto's widow an additional $25,000 for town lots in Avalon and took possession of the Island.

In 1896, William Banning formed the Santa Catalina Island Company, whose stock was owned by five Banning brothers and sisters: William, Hancock, Judge J.B., Katherine, and Anna. He deeded Catalina Island to the Santa Catalina Island Company, and he and his two brothers, Hancock and Judge J.B., "proceeded to make this tiny green speck, first discovered by Cabrillo, into a 'Paradise of the Pacific,' known and loved by sportsmen the world over."

Catalina Becomes a World-Class Playground

The wealthy came by yacht to Catalina to play, avid anglers came to fish, and tourists came to ride stagecoaches and glass bottom boats. During the Banning years, Catalina became a resort known throughout the world.

Many generations of Californians spent their summers on Catalina Island. Choice property was sold to Banning friends, and a number of family compounds sprang up, including the boyhood summer home of George S. Patton, whose grandfather had been the partner of Phineas Banning. Other tourists settled in elaborate encampments under colorful tents consisting of "one or two beds, a wash-stand with drawers, two chairs, two rockers, a strip of carpet, electric lights, and the necessary crockery." Warm days would be spent playing on the beaches; evening memories were made dancing outdoors under Japanese lanterns or singing around campfires.

This July 1, 1893 journal entry typifies the response of many to Catalina:

> *A Paradise of the Pacific – Eureka! I have found IT! IT, thus emphasized, is my Ideal Camping Ground; my Happy Hunting Ground; the Abode of Manitou. Truly IT is Paradise, or the vestibule thereof, which is good enough for me! Catalina Island. . . .My tent is pitched on a high point overlooking the bay, with its scores of dancing boats . . . .My boat floats at her mooring just below, and I, in my Sea-gull's Nest, shall dream fine dreams, and think high and beautiful thoughts. . . .Over all pours a flood of sunshine, which lights the raiment of the hills with a golden splendor. The soft air is elixir, and seems to fill one's whole being with a new life.*

Visitors wanted more than a place to sleep. They wanted things to do, and, during the Banning years, a rich array of leisure pursuits sprang up. . . .

Catalina's Marine Life Draws Visitors

Charles Frederick Holder's passion for marine life was the driving force for many of the leisure pursuits that developed during the Banning years. One of the most popular was the glass bottom boat, which he called "a new and valuable ally to education." Avalon's first glass bottom boat was a rowboat built in 1896. It was inspired by the wooden box with a glass bottom used by fishermen to look at lines that had gotten tangled in the kelp forests and by divers when hunting for abalone. By 1897, a second glass bottom boat was completed. This boat was built using bicycle parts and could be pedaled around the harbor. By 1902, Avalon tourists could ride a 38-foot long sidewheeler glass bottom boat powered by a gasoline motor.

To make these glass bottom boat trips even more exciting, skin divers without diving suits would dart under the boats. One diver became famous for his ability to stay in 56 feet of water for three minutes and fifty-six seconds without any equipment. Much later, after World War II, divers in Navy diving suits would walk along the bottom under the boats talking to passengers via a telephone system. Another post-World War II underwater tourist attraction was the Diving Bell at Casino Point. Tourists were lowered into the ocean in a metal tank with windows to watch the marine life. As visitors obtained their own scuba equipment, the Diving Bell was no longer popular and was dismantled.

Holder also established a sport at Avalon that has become known throughout the world. In 1898, he and six friends founded the Tuna Club, the birthplace of competitive deep-sea fishing. Here, for the

Avalon's glass bottom boats in the late 1800s

first time, strictly defined rules of sport fishing were established. Types and weight of tackle, in addition to the rules of behavior for the angler, were clearly defined. These rules were formulated so that fishing could be a contest of the angler's skill. A foundational assumption of these rules was that they gave the fish a fair chance of survival. According to an article in the *Los Angeles Times*:

> *Holder was horrified to find that men were taking [tuna] on heavy hand lines, almost rope. Many were pulled aboard and thrown away.... [T]he aim of [the Tuna Club] has been to preserve big-game fishing as a sport in which the angler and the boatman is matched against the native cunning and strength of the fish*

The notion of treating fishing as a sport caught on throughout the world. The Tuna Club at Avalon became the international arbitrator of sport fishing rules. Anglers from all over the world looked to Catalina for direction, and, whenever they got the chance, they came to Catalina to fish for tuna, swordfish, and giant black bass. The Tuna Club is still an active organization that has accomplished a

Original Tuna Club, founded in 1898

great deal. It has been instrumental in efforts to conserve game and fish throughout the waters of Southern California and has worked hard to protect California's spawning areas. In 1913, Catalina Island was decreed a fish reservation. The law, drafted by Holder, mandates:

> Every person who takes, catches, or kills any fish except with hook and line in the manner commonly known as angling within three miles of shoreline of Santa Catalina Island, is guilty of a misdemeanor.

Catalina's sealions also became world-famous during the Banning years. Sealions from Seal Rock, at the east end of Catalina, became very valuable. Trainers discovered that Catalina's sealions were the brightest and most trainable in the world. Even today, most performing "seals" (really sealions) in circuses throughout the world trace their ancestry to Catalina Island. Circus trainers visited Catalina regularly during the Banning years. In the early 1900s, a circus act named "The Travillo Brothers" came to Catalina looking for a sealion to augment their act. While there, the family realized that they wanted to leave the circus life and make Catalina their home. By 1906, they had built a distinctive home and trained sealions in the yard while their sons entertained the tourists by diving for coins.

Catalina's Sea Monster

During these years, tourists were delighted, awed, and frightened by talk of a sea monster in Catalina's waters. Observers described an enormous sea serpent much like the famous monster of Loch Ness. It supposedly had a six-foot long head shaped like that of an elephant. Its three-toed tracks in the wet sand measured three feet long and two feet wide. Although there was never any proof accompanying the sightings, a 1941 **National Geographic** article gave its support to Catalina's sea monster tales. According to this article by Dr. J. L. B. Smith, "It is more than likely that there is a real 'sea serpent' [based on] many reports of a huge-bodied, long-necked creature, somewhat resembling the supposedly extinct plesiosaurus."

45

Camp Monrovia, popular summer holiday destination

Catalina's sea serpent added an element of mystery and danger that increased the Island's appeal to visitors from all over the world.

Visitors to Isthmus

A dirt road was built between Avalon and Isthmus. In honor of the proud Banning tradition as Southern California's pioneer stagecoach family, the only travel between the two towns was by stagecoach. William Banning, one of the finest amateur six-in-hand drivers in the United States, occasionally drove these stagecoaches. Tourists who visited Isthmus stayed in a tent village on the beach.

In 1910, Judge J. B. Banning built a large hacienda on a knoll overlooking Isthmus. Guests of the Bannings were lavishly entertained at this hacienda. Over the years, Banning's home at Isthmus was the scene of numerous hunting parties and social functions. The rich and famous were frequently brought from the mainland on a Banning yacht to party at the hacienda. In later years Hollywood stars, acting in one of the many movies filmed at Isthmus, stayed at

Banning's hacienda.

In 1941, the hacienda was taken over by the U. S. Coast Guard as quarters for their officers. After World War II, it was used for a variety of purposes, including a girls' camp, a dude ranch, and a hunting lodge. In 1987, Doug Bombard, a lifelong resident of Catalina, began restoring Banning's hacienda. Today, it is a beautifully restored bed and breakfast called the Banning House Lodge.

Communication Breakthroughs

Catalina's isolation had always given the Island an air of romance and mystery. During the Banning years, it became evident that her isolation offered the United States opportunities to pioneer some exciting new communication technologies. Catalina was perfectly located for such experimentation—so near and yet so far from the mainland. In 1902, the world's first commercial wireless telegraph station was built in Avalon where the Chimes Tower now stands. By 1903, Catalina had its first locally printed newspaper. This paper was unusual because the *Los Angeles Times* transmitted the news to the paper each day by the wireless telegraph.

Communication history continued even after the Bannings sold Catalina. By 1919, the world's first wireless telephone was installed at Avalon. Engineers from all over the world came to study it. People waited in lines for hours to call their friends, using this fascinating new way to communicate. This early wireless telephone system had one weakness—all conversations could be monitored by anyone listening to their radios at home. (Eventually, these wireless telephone conversations were scrambled to provide privacy to customers.) This wireless telephone service was replaced by cable in 1923, when Pacific Telephone laid 300-ton cables along the ocean floor to the mainland.

Another communication breakthrough touched Catalina when the world's first commercial microwave telephone system was installed in 1946. Although this was new technology to civilians, microwave telephones had been used during World War II. Catalina was the showcase selected to test this new product for peacetime applications.

By 1921, Catalina had its first radio station. It was a simple crystal set constructed by Lawrence Mott at his home. This station made radio history when it was the only station able to maintain contact with the 1922-23 McMillan Expedition to the North Pole for a full three weeks.

Hardships Challenge the Bannings

The Bannings owned Catalina for twenty-seven years. During these years they did much to develop Catalina into a resort and an angler's paradise. Unfortunately, these years were not idyllic for the Bannings. When they purchased Catalina, they had the transportation monopoly to the Island. When competing ferry companies began bringing tourists to Catalina, the Bannings were outraged and began a nine-year battle against these competitors. They erected barbed-wire fences to stop tourists who had used competing ferries

The fire of 1915 devastated much of Avalon.

from landing. Ferrymen from rival companies were often seen fighting on the beaches of Avalon.

In an attempt to establish order, the Avalon Freeholder's Improvement Association was organized. Although this group was unsuccessful in controlling the embattled competitors, it was successful in building a public pier, now known as the Pleasure Pier, which allowed all ferry services access to the Island.

Another concern during the Banning years was Catalina's inadequate water supply. It was not until a disastrous fire leveled much of Avalon that the Bannings were forced to face Catalina's water problems. In November 1915, a fire destroyed over one-third of Avalon. The cause of the fire was never discovered. Some believe this fire was set intentionally to bankrupt the Bannings and force them to sell Catalina If this was true, the arsons were successful. As a result of this fire, the Bannings lost over a million dollars and began their financial decline. One positive result of the fire is that the Bannings installed an electric plant that pumped saltwater by pipe throughout the town to give Avalon some much-needed fire protection.

Hotel St. Catherine at Descanso,
traces of which still remain

Avalon's Hotel Metropole was destroyed by the fire. The Bannings were convinced that a fine hotel was necessary to Catalina's future. Soon after the flames had died, the Bannings began planning a new, lavish hotel—the Hotel St. Catherine. The lot they selected is the site of today's Casino. They blasted away a huge rock, called Big Sugarloaf Rock, to clear enough room for the hotel. After the blasting had been completed, the site was rejected in favor of a lot on Descanso Bay, a cove north of Avalon Harbor. The St. Catherine was completed in 1918, and gala celebrations marked its opening.

The cost of the hotel, in addition to their large losses in the 1915 fire, was too much for the Bannings. In 1919, they sold Catalina to **William Wrigley, Jr.**, Catalina's most famous and richest owner. Wrigley had a vision for Catalina and the energy, money, and commitment to make these visions a reality. Catalina was entering an era that was to shape and change her future significantly.

Home to Ranchers

While Catalina was being purchased by entrepreneurs and transformed into the playground of the world, ranchers were making the Island their home. Under the assumption that Catalina was unclaimed United States territory, they invoked Squatter's Rights, the law that allowed citizens to own land without purchasing it by cultivating it and building a home.

The Ranching Families

Based upon this assumption, a number of ranchers had established homes and viable enterprises on Catalina Island by the middle of the 19th century. Many of the coves and landings are named for these ranchers, who used them to transport their cattle during these ranching years.

One of the best known of these ranchers was **Captain William Howland**. He and his wife settled on Catalina Island in 1858. They prospered by raising cattle and sheep and soon had a herd of more than 3,000 sheep. They built a comfortable home overlooking a cove on the west end of Catalina that is still known as Howland's Landing. A baby, their second son, was born there in 1865. This boy is believed to have been the first non-Native Islander born on Catalina.

Another rancher, **Ben Weston**, settled near Little Harbor and built himself a stone home on what is still known as Ben Weston's Beach. His herd of sheep soon numbered 2,000.

The bachelor **Johnson** brothers, **John** and **Charles**, had arrived in 1854 and by the 1870s owned 3,000 sheep and 100 mares and colts, in addition to a flourishing fruit and vegetable garden. **Frank**

Whittley lived at Isthmus. He had arrived from Mexico in 1850 with a herd of sheep, his four-year-old son, and a seven-year old youngster named **Joe Presciado**. Joe, who soon earned the nickname "Mexican Joe," was "wild and climbing and always after goats." Joe spent the rest of his life on Catalina Island and knew the Island very well. According to Joe, in an interview by the *Los Angeles Morning Herald* on October 30, 1903, "If there is a tree on the Island I don't know, it must have grown last night." As an adult, Joe guided goat hunters around the Island and rowed fishermen around Catalina.

In addition to these ranching families, an entrepreneur known as Dr. Creal, came to Catalina from Los Angeles with the express purpose of supplying goat meat to the hungry gold prospectors in San Francisco. Within three years, he had 25,000 goats and was earning $4 per goat. Legend has it that some of these goats were so large that their hides resembled that of a grizzly bear.

When the Union Army occupied Catalina and banished all prospectors, ranchers were allowed to stay. Each contributed to the war effort in one way or another. The Johnson brothers furnished the army with beef and mutton. Howland's well provided their water. Although Howland was forced to take down his fence between Isthmus and Cat Harbor, he convinced the Army to let him reassemble his fence on a nearby hillside so that his flock could not wander into the Army garrison. The Army took Whittley's corrals and used them to store food for their animals. When the Army left a year later, the ranching families were able to resume their routine on their island paradise—for awhile.

James Lick versus the Ranchers

When developers began to compete for ownership of Catalina, the lifestyle of the ranching families was threatened. The first owners bought and sold Catalina without seriously disrupting the lives of the ranchers. When James Lick purchased Catalina, the lives of the ranching families began to change. Lick planned to make a fortune by selling Catalina to foreign investors as a rich gold field. He was convinced that the ranchers were illegally squatting on his private property and believed that he must rid Catalina of ranchers before his dream of wealth could become a reality. In 1868, he began litigation against the ranchers and the few miners who remained on the Island. He insisted they were illegally squatting on his property and planned to evict all of them.

The ranchers petitioned for their rights, and Lick maneuvered to evict them. The legal battle raged for four years, until in 1872, the courts upheld Lick's claim. The ranchers had lost. The process to evict the ranchers began.

By 1874, the ranchers were still living on Catalina. By this time, an aging Lick had turned over all of his holdings to a trust administered by the University of California. Howland, one of the prominent ranchers, offered the trustees $50,000 for the Island. His offer was rejected. Nevertheless, despite threats by the trustees, the ranchers remained on Catalina.

Cattle drive at White's Landing

By 1887, James Lick had died, and the trustees of his estate had granted grazing rights to the three prominent Catalina ranchers who remained on the Island: Howland, Harris, and Whittley. These ranchers had won the right to remain in their homes, and, after many years of conflict, ranching was finally declared a legitimate occupation on Catalina Island.

Even after Catalina's pioneer ranching families had left, some ranching continued. In 1894, the Banning brothers leased the grazing rights to the Mauer Cattle Company. In exchange for the lease, the Bannings got one-quarter of the profit. Many of these sheep lived long after this lease expired. As late as 1923, San Pedro commercial fishermen were still slaughtering large numbers of the sheep left on the Island and leaving their skins on the beaches.

Even today, a variety of ranching activities continue. These include the thriving bison herd that freely roams the Island and the world-famous Arabian horse farm, El Escondido. Although the original families no longer live on Catalina Island, it is easy to picture them when one looks at the undeveloped, unspoiled hills of Catalina where their herds once roamed.

Sheep grazing on the Island

Wrigley's Catalina (1919-1975)

William Wrigley, Jr.'s purchase of Catalina in 1919 marked the end of nearly seven decades during which Catalina had been bought and sold by a wide variety of entrepreneurs.

Few held on to her for very long. Only the Bannings had kept her long enough to make a significant impact on the course of her development. It was under the ownership of the Wrigleys that Catalina became what she is today—a wonderful place to live (for those few who can) and an idyllic holiday spot for the millions who visit every year. The Wrigleys, William, Jr. (until his death in 1932), and his son, Philip, put a great deal of energy and millions of dollars of their personal wealth into making Catalina a grand place to live and to visit.

Water, Housing, and Jobs for Residents

Although headlines were made by the tourist activities they supported, the Wrigleys put a tremendous amount of effort into making Catalina Island a better place for its permanent residents to live.

Water

Water on Catalina had always been a problem. During most of the Banning years, water had been brought over in the holds of the two passenger ships making frequent trips to the Island. As the resident population grew and greater numbers of tourists visited Catalina each year, supplying adequate water became a serious problem.

During the Wrigley years, Catalina finally got a dependable source of water. The Wrigleys spent over a million dollars drilling wells, digging

William Wrigley, Jr.

tunnels, building a dam, and constructing water storage reservoirs. As a result, Catalina has a large reservoir named Thompson Dam. Completed in 1923, it originally held 100 million gallons of water; it has since been expanded to hold 326 million gallons.

A $3,000,000 desalination plant capable of producing 132,000 gallons of water a day has also been built as a back-up system for those years of drought. This system gave Catalina residents and visitors a plentiful and consistent supply of fresh water and ended Catalina's water worries. The sewage system and fire department still use saltwater to flush toilets and to extinguish fires.

Homes

Wrigley wanted Catalina to be a good place for people to live, and he spent much effort and money trying to establish housing and jobs for residents. Catalina's shortage of affordable housing was the easiest of these concerns to solve. In addition to providing lots to residents at affordable prices, Wrigley built the Atwater Hotel to provide affordable housing options for residents unable to purchase lots. The Atwater Arcade, which currently houses shops and the Post Office, was built as a cafeteria to feed those living in the hotel.

Jobs

Providing employment and dependable sources of income for Catalina residents proved to be far more difficult. Although many residents were employed during the summer supporting Catalina's growing tourist industry, Wrigley wanted year-round jobs for Catalina residents. Construction provided one viable source of employment, but Wrigley sought to establish additional industries to provide employment for residents, as well as profit for himself. For a time, it appeared that mining would be the answer, but, when

Hotel Atwater and Arcade

mineral prices dropped, mining was no longer profitable.

One successful enterprise Wrigley established was the Catalina Pottery Company (1927). Wrigley discovered Catalina's clay by accident. There are two stories about this discovery:

1) Some say that he backed his car too near one of Catalina's hills and got stuck in the mud. He was intrigued by the elasticity of the mud that stuck to his tires. He had it analyzed and found it to be a high-quality clay.

2) Others believe a 1932 **Popular Science Magazine** article full of rather flamboyant praise for Wrigley's benevolence:

> *"Like a fairy story out of real life is the tale of a Catalina Island quarry owner so interested in the health of his workmen that he installed a system to shield their lungs from the deadly effects of breathing the dust-laden air. Just as those who do good deeds in fables receive unexpected and fitting rewards, so did the modern benefactor in this true story. For the despised dust, sucked from the excavations through pipes and collected in a bin for disposal, was found to be unsurpassed as a material for making beautiful pottery. Now a thriving industry has grown up around the discovery and scores of craftsmen are engaged in the unique occupation of making pottery from the air."*

However it was discovered, it was clear that Catalina's resources provided some promising minerals for making pottery. In addition to providing employment for residents, the pottery paving bricks, drainage tiles, roof tiles, flooring tiles, chimney pots, and flowerpots that were produced were in high demand on the Island. Large quantities of these products were needed both for new construction and to replace pottery broken during Catalina's fierce winter storms.

By 1930, Wrigley expanded the Catalina Pottery Company products to include decorative pottery and tiles. He hired resident artisans and brought others from the mainland. The resulting pottery, according to A. W. Friedley, the author of **Catalina Pottery**, "was a marvelous mixture of styles and unique colors that are outstanding even today." Catalina pottery also produced a clear bell-like ring when tapped. To capitalize on this unusual attribute of his pottery, Wrigley held afternoon "pottery" concerts at his Wild Bird Park.

The Catalina Pottery Company was successful—so successful that it threatened to become a major competitor to the powerful Gladding McBean Pottery on the mainland. In 1937, five years after the death of William Wrigley, Jr., Gladding McBean bought the Catalina Pottery Company and moved all production to the mainland.

And, so ended a promising attempt to create dependable, year-round employment for residents. Despite Wrigley's efforts, industries on Catalina were not to thrive, and employment continued to be seasonal and dependent upon serving the needs of tourists.

Catalina's Famous Author

Some residents generated their own sources of income when they came to Catalina Island. Zane Grey was one of the many artists and entrepreneurs who flourished on Catalina Island. In 1924, Grey, an Ohio author of eighty-nine adventure books about the American West, built his home on the hill near the Chimes Tower. His home was modeled after a Hopi Indian pueblo. It had a log mantle over the fireplace and was furnished with a hand-hewn upright piano. He had brought the teak beams on his ceilings from Tahiti on his yacht. Today, this unique home is a bed and breakfast, the Pueblo.

Zane Grey loved Catalina. In **What the Open Means to Me**, he shared this love:

> I used to climb the mountain trail that overlooked the Pacific and here a thousand times I shut my eyes and gave myself over to the sensorial perceptions.... It is an environment that means enchantment to me. Sea and mountain! Breeze and roar of surf! ... I could write here and be at peace.

In addition to his homes and his books, Grey made an unexpected

59

permanent impact on Catalina Island. While planning to film one of his Westerns, *The Vanishing American*, in 1924 bison were brought to the Island to enhance its Western look. Although experts agree that the Island was not selected as the location for this movie, the fourteen bison were too much trouble to round up and were left on the Island. By 1934, the original herd had increased to 19 and 30 additional bison had been imported from Colorado to supplement them. Today, a large herd of between 400 and 500 bison delight visitors. Their numbers are watched carefully. When the herd gets too large, some are sent to the mainland to be slaughtered, butchered, frozen, and flown back to Catalina to be sold as buffalo burgers and buffalo chili in local restaurants.

The Tourists Came

While Wrigley may not have been able to establish the industries he wanted to employ the residents, he certainly was successful making Catalina a world-class tourist resort. Wrigley said:

> There is to be nothing of Coney Island flavor about Santa Catalina. It would be unthinkable to mar the beauty of such a spot with roller coasters and the like. . . .(Catalina was developed) to put within reach of the rank and file of the United States – the people to whom I owe my prosperity – a playground where they can enjoy themselves to the utmost, at such a reasonable figure of expense that all can participate in its benefits.

He succeeded. For $10, they got round-trip transportation from Los Angeles, a night at the luxurious Hotel St. Catherine, four meals, and a trip on a glass bottom boat. As an alternate to the hotel, Wrigley built the Island Villas to replace the tent communities that had been multiplying each summer. These villas were small, canvas-topped bungalows where families could stay inexpensively.

Wrigley also made it easy for visitors to build summer houses. When Wrigley purchased Catalina, many had been renting twenty-foot lots with tents and makeshift cottages on them for decades.

They had been coming to Catalina every summer to spend their holiday on their tiny rented lot. Wrigley offered to let them buy these lots at a reasonable price and encouraged them to build summer homes. Many did. They were glad to have a permanent place on Catalina. Wrigley was glad to have homes built in place of the tents and temporary cottages.

And They Played . . .

While on Catalina, the things they could do! They could dance and watch movies in the extraordinary Casino. They could visit the Wild Bird Park and Rancho Escondido, the Wrigley's Arabian Horse Ranch. They could watch the Chicago Cubs in spring training. They could cheer contestants in one of Wrigley's aquatic races. They could wander Avalon's streets, listening to troubadours dressed as early California settlers, and they could watch the Hollywood stars as they worked and as they played.

Dance Pavilion at Avalon

Catalina's Casino

A mere two years after Wrigley had purchased Catalina, he built a dance pavilion. By 1928, seven years after the completion of this dance pavilion, Wrigley decided that it was inadequate and tore it down. Only its dome was recycled to become the giant bird cage of his Wild Bird Park. He replaced it with the Casino, Catalina's most famous landmark. The Casino is an extraordinary building. It was the first completely circular building built in modern times. The patio floor tile, glazed wall tile, and roof tile were all made on the Island at the Catalina Pottery Company. It was the recipient of the Honor Award from the Southern California Chapter of the American Institute of Architects as "one of the outstanding architectural accomplishments."

It was built to serve as a theater on the main floor and a ballroom and a promenade on the upper level. Its height equals that of a twelve-story building, and the 20,000 square foot ballroom can accommodate 3,000 dancers. Its dance floor is made of seven hardwoods on cork. During the Big Band era, many of the famous orchestras, including Kay Kyser and Benny Goodman, came to Avalon's Casino to perform.

The theater, with a capacity of 1,200, was the first theater in the world acoustically engineered to show movies. It had an extraordinary organ to accompany the silent movies, which has recently been renovated. During Hollywood's heyday, movie tycoons, including Cecil B. De Mille, Louis B. Mayer, and Samuel Goldwyn, frequently came by yacht to Avalon to preview their newest productions in the Casino's theater.

Today, it stands watch over Avalon Harbor and can be seen by visitors who are still many miles out to sea. It is used as a movie theater and a museum. Thousands of visitors tour Wrigley's famous Casino each year. In addition to its use as a center of entertainment on Catalina Island, it is also the Island's designated civil defense shelter. It is large enough to accommodate Catalina's entire year-round population. Within its walls is stored enough food and water for all of Catalina's residents for two weeks.

Wild Bird Park

Wrigley used the dome from the old dance pavilion in an unexpected way. He used it to create the world's largest bird cage for a Wild Bird Park he created at the site of the Island's junkyard. The recycled dome created a bird cage that was 90 feet high and 115 feet in diameter. This park was well known and visited by most of the tourists visiting Catalina during the Wrigley years. Reduced in size during World War II, the Wild Bird Park never returned to its original grandeur. When it closed in 1966, the birds were sold to the Los Angeles Zoo. Today, as you wander the backroads of Avalon, you can see this extraordinary, abandoned bird cage.

Mt. Ada

During these years, a home was built that has become a Catalina landmark. In 1921, Wrigley built his home on Mt. Ada on a large estate overlooking Avalon Bay. His wife, Ada, selected its site, because she felt that it was the perfect spot to watch the sun rise and set. In 1978, the estate was donated to the University of Southern California and was used by the University for conferences for sev-

The Inn at Mt. Ada

eral years. In 1985, Wrigley's home was restored and converted to a luxurious bed and breakfast called "The Inn at Mt. Ada." Additionally, in 1963, Philip K. Wrigley and his family donated 45 acres at Big Fisherman Cove near the Isthmus to the University of Southern California to build a marine science research center. Today, the Marine Science Center includes laboratories, classrooms, a library, dormitories, dining facilities, and a diving center, including boats and a hyperbaric chamber.

Rancho Escondido

By 1929, Philip K. Wrigley, William Wrigley, Jr.'s son, had begun planning the family's Arabian Horse Ranch, "Rancho Escondido," meaning "the Hidden Ranch." The birthplace of horses that have won hundreds of national awards, this ranch is still thriving. Thousands of visitors visit the ranch each year to see its incredible horses.

Chicago Cubs

During the Wrigley Years, Catalina became famous throughout the world as the spring training paradise of the Chicago Cubs. For twenty-six years, they came every spring. With the Cubs came hosts of sport writers. When there was nothing new to say about the Cubs, writers filled their columns with praises for Catalina Island. During the Banning years, anglers from all over the world had gotten to know Catalina well. The anglers never forgot the Island, but now sports fans everywhere knew a lot about Catalina Island, too.

Aquatic Races

In 1927, Wrigley organized two aquatic races called the "Wrigley Ocean Marathons". The less noteworthy of these was a summer rowboat race in which 49 contestants rowed from Long Beach to Avalon. The winner completed the race in five hours and won $1,000.

The more famous of these "Wrigley Ocean Marathons" was also held in 1927. January was the month selected for the race, so that the world would notice Catalina's mild weather in the middle of winter. $25,000 was offered to the first swimmer to complete the 22-mile race from Isthmus to Point Vicente. If this prize were won by a man, the first woman finisher would also be awarded $15,000. This event is believed to have received more press coverage than any other aquatic event ever held.

One-hundred and three swimmers entered the race. Three people in a rowboat accompanied each swimmer—a trainer, an observer, and an oarsman. The observer was there to make sure that all of the rules of the race were obeyed. Each observer stayed with a swimmer for eighty minutes before being assigned to another swimmer. These changes were considered to be necessary to ensure that

Chicago Cubs at spring training

observers did not have time to become so sympathetic to a swimmer that rules would be disregarded. A powerboat was in attendance, with a physician, emergency equipment, and friends of the swimmers.

Of the 103 contestants, only one completed the race. The winner was George Young, a 17-year-old who had bicycled from his home in Canada to compete. He swam for 15 hours and 46 minutes in water temperatures ranging from 56 to 62 degrees. Dragged down by kelp, he staggered ashore at 3:08 a.m. After George won, one of the two women who were still trying to complete the race, Margaret Hauser, refuse to give up. By 6:30 a.m., she was dragged by force from the water. Both of these women were given $2500 for their tenacity and bravery.

The "Wrigley Ocean Marathons" were never repeated. Although sports enthusiasts tried to convince Wrigley to stage the events again, he refused. He felt that he would be tempting fate to try the races again. Conditions had been good, and no one had been hurt. He was unwilling to take the chance again. Additionally, the swimming marathon has cost him the sizeable sum of $155,000 to sponsor.

Although Wrigley never again sponsored his marathons, many have swam across the Channel to Catalina. Greta Andersen, a noncompetitive swimmer, made one of the more extraordinary crossings. In October 1958, she swam to and from Catalina in 26 hours. She started from Emerald Bay and arrived at Pt. Vincente 10 hours and 22 minutes later. After a 27-minute rest, she began her swim back to Emerald Bay. She reached Emerald Bay fifteen hours and 36 minutes later.

Philip K. Wrigley

In 1932, William Wrigley, Jr. died, and his son **Philip K. Wrigley** inherited Catalina. He transformed Avalon into a romanticized combination of the Old West and Hollywood. He believed that:

> *Being an island we can control a definite plan over a period of years, unhampered by outside commercialism... [W]e may be able to make all of Catalina Island a monument to early California.*

He planted the beachfront with 50-year-old palm trees and olive trees he had shipped from the mainland. Tons of sand were brought

Philip K. Wrigley

by barge to cover Avalon's natural pebblestone beach. Avalon's shops were given facelifts. Troubadours, dressed as early California settlers, played everywhere—on the streets, on the beaches, and even on the steamers bringing tourists to Catalina. Even the stevedores did not escape Avalon's fantasyland, for they, too, were in costume.

Catalina's Celebrities

For many years, Catalina was a favorite work and play spot for Hollywood's rich and famous. Charlie Chaplin, John Wayne, Stan Laurel, Oliver Hardy, Tom Mix, David Niven, and Errol Flynn were among the famous who played well at Catalina Island. A number of movies were filmed at Isthmus, especially those with south sea settings. These include:

Mutiny on the Bounty   *King of Kings*   *Old Ironsides*
Treasure Island   *The SeaWitch*   *McHale's Navy*
Guadalcanal Diary   *MacArthur*

Cat Harbor, across the narrow arm of land from Isthmus, had its own pirate ship, **Ning Po**, moored and ready to star in its next movie. This ship was a well-known junk sailed by pirates in Asian seas. It had journeyed from China under its own sail and rested at Cat Harbor for many years as a tearoom, museum, and movie prop. Eventually it was abandoned and sank in 1938 during a severe storm. In addition to **Ning Po**, the Isthmus and Cat Harbor had a fleet of old sailing ships which were used for nautical shots needed for historical movie scenes. None of these ships remain. Eventually, all of these vessels were blown up in battle scenes or disintegrated and sank.

When they were not working, the Hollywood stars played at Catalina Island. For twelve years, from 1945 until his death in 1957, Humphrey Bogart and his wife, Lauren Bacall, had owned **Santana**, a 55-foot Sparkman-Stevens sailboat. They spent many weekends on their yacht exploring the waters of Southern California and frequently anchored at either White's Landing or Cherry Cove. Certain weekends were for guys only, for, according to Bogart, "The trouble with having dames along is that you can't pee over the side." On those weekends, he and his all-male crew swam, drank, and feasted on illegally caught local lobster.

The women were always invited on Fourth of July. One Fourth, Bogie and Bacall sailed to Cherry Cove with their sailing companions, David Niven and his wife Hjordis. In his memoirs, David Niven recalled this Catalina weekend:

> *Frank Sinatra rafted-up alongside us in a chartered motor cruiser with several beautiful girls and a small piano. After dinner, with Jimmy Van Heusen accompanying him, Sinatra began to sing. He sang all night. There were many more yachts in Cherry Cove that weekend, and by two in the morning, under a full moon, Santana was surrounded by an audience sitting in dozens of dinghies and rubber tenders of every shape and size. Frank sang till the moon and stars paled in the dawn sky. Only then did he stop, and only then did the awed and grateful audience paddle silently home.*

The *Ning Po*, used in many Catalina movies

Airline Service to Catalina Island

Most people who came to Catalina arrived in a variety of boats, both large and small, powered by motor or sail. It took many years for Catalina to have regular airline service. Catalina Island was the destination of the first over-the-water flight when Glenn Martin (founder of Martin Aviation) flew from Balboa Peninsula to Avalon in 1912 in the plane that he had built in his garage in Santa Ana. Nevertheless, it took Catalina many years to get an airport and regular flights to the mainland.

The first passenger flights began in 1919 but lasted only two months. The service was cancelled due to high costs. Another pilot tried to make a profit providing trans-channel service in 1920 but found short sightseeing flights over the Island to be more profitable.

"Pocket" airport at Hamilton Beach

Pacific Marine Airways began operating two seaplanes to Catalina in 1920 but gave up the operation after three unprofitable seasons. In 1925, they tried again but still could not make the seaplane service profitable enough. Even Goodyear tried to operate a passenger blimp service to Catalina. Again, the service cost too much, and the profits simply were not there.

In 1931, Philip K. Wrigley organized the Wilmington-Catalina Air Line, Ltd. He built an unusual airport at Hamilton Beach, just north of the Hotel St. Catherine. The ocean was its landing field. Planes landed at the foot of the mountain and at the mouth of a narrow canyon on a ramp. This ramp ran onto a turntable that turned the airplanes around so that they were ready to take off again. It is believed that Philip K. Wrigley's method of turning airplanes around was unique in the world. Before World War II, construction of a more traditional airport in the interior of the Island was begun, but it was not completed until 1946. To build its landing strip, the peaks of two mountains had to be leveled.

World War II

Catalina changed almost immediately after Pearl Harbor was bombed in December 1941. As an outpost in the Chanel, it was considered to be both vulnerable to Japanese attack and a prime training ground for American Armed Forces. From 1941-45, Catalina was closed to the public. The Hotel St. Catherine was converted into a school for Merchant Marine cooks. The Catalina Island Yacht Club became classrooms to train Coast Guard, Office of Strategic Services (O.S.S.), and Signal Corps recruits. A battery of anti-aircraft guns was mounted on the roof of the Casino. Construction on the airport stopped immediately, and the partially constructed landing strips were covered with barbed wire to stop the Japanese from landing and attacking.

After World War II, it took two years and over a million dollars to return the facilities, converted by the military, back to their former peacetime uses. The Hotel St. Catherine never regained its splendor and was torn down in 1965. Some of the other facilities, including the Atwater Hotel and the Casino, were leased to individual entrepreneurs. Despite these changes, as soon as Catalina was opened up again to the public, visitors flocked back. They had missed their Island during the war years and were now ready to play again.

U.S. Maritime Service trainees at Avalon

Catalina Island Conservancy

For decades, many assumed that Catalina Island would become a bedroom community for rapidly growing metropolitan Los Angeles. In 1975, the Wrigley family ensured that this would not happen. To protect the natural wonders of this island paradise, they formed the Santa Catalina Island Conservancy and deeded their 42,000 acres

The St. Catherine, demolished after WW II

to this trust. This major shift in ownership changed the course of Catalina's future forever. The formation of the Santa Catalina Island Conservancy ensured the preservation of the Island and averted its fate as a Los Angeles suburb.

The mandate of the Conservancy is to preserve and protect Catalina and its magnificent natural heritage. The task of the Conservancy is enormous and includes:

-*Managing fifty miles of shoreline*
-*Overseeing over 40,000 acres of land*
-*Operating an airport*
-*Monitoring a bison herd*
-*Maintaining over 100 miles of roads*
-*Overseeing ecological restoration and scientific research*
-*Welcoming over 1,000,000 visitors each year*
-*Protecting biological communities found nowhere else*
-*Guarding a treasure trove of historical and archeological sites*

The numerous and complex activities of the Conservancy are funded from a variety of sources including camping leases, mooring operations, donations, and membership dues. As it uses no government or tax funds, it is always actively seeking new members and donations to continue its important work.

Today, Catalina remains largely uninhabited and rich with natural wonders. Visitors can tour Avalon by foot or by golf carts. To explore the rest of Catalina Island, one can ride horseback, hike with a special permit, or can anchor their boat in one of its wonderful coves. There are neither freeways, nor shopping centers, nor chain restaurants. Just a wonderful island paradise filled with a rich historical heritage.

I hope you have enjoyed this introduction to Catalina Island. If you want to learn more about Catalina's story, visit the folks at the Catalina Island Museum in the Casino. They will gladly take over as your Catalina time travel adventure guides. Happy traveling!

Index

Sources

HarborTown Histories are designed to introduce you to the fascinating stories of grand towns rich with history. Hopefully Catalina's story has given you just the glimpse you need to want to learn more about this wonderful island. If I have done my job, you will want to read more. You may want to begin your journey with these books . . .

Guide to Catalina and California's Channel Islands by Chicki Mallan, Moon Publications, Chico, California, 3rd. Edition, 1990.

The Catalina Story by Alma Overholt, First Printing, 1962, edited and updated, 1971 by Jack Sargent, Curator of the Catalina Island Museum. Published by the Catalina Island Musuem.

The Ranch that was Robbins' – Santa Catalina Island, California: A Source Book by Adelaide LeMert Doran, The Arthur H. Clark Company, Publisher and Booksellers, Second Printing, 1964.

Santa Catalina Island – Its Magic, People, and History by William Sanford White, with Stephen Kern Tice, White Limited Editions, 1997.

Winston Churchill with catch-of-the-day, 1929.

Turn-of-the-century photo-op.